BERNSTEIN FOR SINGERS

10 SONGS

T0065955

To access companion recorded accompaniments online, visit:
www.halleonard.com/mylibrary

Enter Code
6126-5947-5684-1027

ISBN 978-1-4803-6449-3

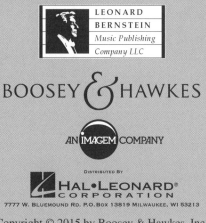

LEONARD
BERNSTEIN
Music Publishing
Company LLC

BOOSEY & HAWKES

AN IMAGEM COMPANY

DISTRIBUTED BY

HAL•LEONARD®
CORPORATION
7777 W. BLUEMOUND RD. P.O. BOX 13819 MILWAUKEE, WI 53213

www.leonardbernstein.com
www.boosey.com
www.halleonard.com

LEONARD BERNSTEIN
August 25, 1918 - October 14, 1990

Leonard Bernstein was born in Lawrence, Massachusetts. He took piano lessons as a boy and attended the Garrison and Boston Latin Schools. At Harvard University he studied with Walter Piston, Edward Burlingame-Hill, and A. Tillman Merritt, among others. Before graduating in 1939 he made an unofficial conducting debut with his own incidental music to the Aristophanes play *The Birds*, and directed and performed in Marc Blitzstein's *The Cradle Will Rock*. Subsequently, at the Curtis Institute of Music in Philadelphia, Bernstein studied piano with Isabella Vengerova, conducting with Fritz Reiner, and orchestration with Randall Thompson.

In 1940 Bernstein studied at the Boston Symphony Orchestra's newly created summer institute, Tanglewood, with the orchestra's conductor, Serge Koussevitzky. Bernstein later became Koussevitzky's conducting assistant. He made a sensational conducting debut with the New York Philharmonic in 1943. Bernstein became Music Director of the orchestra in 1958. From then until 1969 he led more concerts with the orchestra than any previous conductor. He subsequently held the lifetime title of Laureate Conductor, making frequent guest appearances with the orchestra. More than half of Bernstein's 400-plus recordings were made with the New York Philharmonic.

Bernstein traveled the world as a conductor. Immediately after World War II, in 1946, he conducted in London and at the International Music Festival in Prague. In 1947 he conducted in Tel Aviv, beginning a relationship with Israel that lasted until his death. In 1953 Bernstein was the first American to conduct opera at the Teatro alla Scala in Milan, in Cherubini's *Medea* with Maria Callas.

Beyond many distinguished achievements as a composer of concert works, Bernstein also wrote a one-act opera, *Trouble in Tahiti* (1952), and its sequel, the opera *A Quiet Place* (1983). He collaborated with choreographer Jerome Robbins on three major ballets: *Fancy Free* (1944), and *Facsimile* (1946) for American Ballet Theater, and *Dybbuk* (1974) for the New York City Ballet. Bernstein composed the score for the award-winning film *On the Waterfront* (1954) and incidental music for the Broadway play *The Lark* (1955).

Bernstein contributed substantially to the Broadway musical stage. He collaborated with Betty Comden and Adolph Green on *On the Town* (1944) and *Wonderful Town* (1953). For *Peter Pan* (1950) he penned his own lyrics to songs and also composed incidental music. In collaboration with Richard Wilbur, Lillian Hellman and others he wrote *Candide* (1956). Other versions of *Candide* were written in association with Hugh Wheeler, Stephen Sondheim and other lyricists. In 1957 he collaborated with Jerome Robbins, Stephen Sondheim and Arthur Laurents on the landmark musical *West Side Story*, which was made into an Academy Award-winning film. Bernstein also wrote the Broadway musical *1600 Pennsylvania Avenue* (1976) with lyricist Alan Jay Lerner.

In 1985 the National Academy of Recording Arts and Sciences honored Bernstein with the Lifetime Achievement Grammy Award. He won eleven Emmy Awards in his career. His televised concert and lecture series were launched with the "Omnibus" program in 1954, followed by the extraordinary "Young People's Concerts with the New York Philharmonic," which began in 1958 and extended over fourteen seasons. Among his many appearances on the PBS series "Great Performances" was the acclaimed eleven-part "Bernstein's Beethoven." In 1989 Bernstein and others commemorated the 1939 invasion of Poland in a worldwide telecast from Warsaw.

Bernstein's writings were published in *The Joy of Music* (1959), *Leonard Bernstein's Young People's Concerts* (1961), *The Infinite Variety of Music* (1966), and *Findings* (1982). Each has been widely translated. He gave six lectures at Harvard University in 1972-1973 as the Charles Eliot Norton Professor of Poetry. These lectures were subsequently published and televised as *The Unanswered Question*.

Bernstein received many honors. He was elected in 1981 to the American Academy of Arts and Letters, which gave him its Gold Medal. The National Fellowship Award in 1985 applauded his life-long support of humanitarian causes. He received the MacDowell Colony's Gold Medal; medals from the Beethoven Society and the Mahler Gesellschaft; the Handel Medallion, New York City's highest honor for the arts; a Tony award (1969) for Distinguished Achievement in the Theater; and dozens of honorary degrees and awards from colleges and universities. Bernstein was presented ceremonial keys to the cities of Oslo, Vienna, Bersheeva, and the village of Bernstein, Austria, among others. National honors came from Italy, Israel, Mexico, Denmark, Germany (the Great Merit Cross), and France (Chevalier, Officer and Commandeur of the Legion d'Honneur). Bernstein received the Kennedy Center Honors in 1980.

In 1990 Bernstein received the Praemium Imperiale, an international prize created in 1988 by the Japan Arts Association and awarded for lifetime achievement in the arts. He used the $100,000 prize to establish initiatives in the arts and education, principally the Leonard Bernstein Center for Artful Learning.

Bernstein was the father of three children — Jamie, Alexander and Nina — and enjoyed the arrival of his first two grandchildren, Francisca and Evan.

TABLE OF CONTENTS

4   Notes on the Shows and Songs

MASS
9   A Simple Song* [3]

ON THE TOWN
17   I Feel Like I'm Not Out of Bed Yet [3]
20   Lonely Town [3]
25   Lucky to Be Me [4]
30   Some Other Time [3]

WEST SIDE STORY
33   Cool [2]
36   Jet Song [1]
39   Maria [3]

WONDERFUL TOWN
44   It's Love [2]
50   A Quiet Girl [4]

Pianists on the recording: [1] Brian Dean; [2] Chris Ruck; [3] Jamie Johns; [4] Richard Walters;
* Sonora Slocum, flute

Notes on the Shows and Songs

MASS

A theatre piece for singers, players and dancers. Music by Leonard Bernstein. Text from the liturgy of the Roman mass, with additional texts by Stephen Schwartz and Leonard Bernstein. First performance: September 8, 1971, Kennedy Center, Washington, D.C. Directed by Gordon Davidson; choreographed by Alvin Ailey; conducted by Maurice Peress.

Selection:

A Simple Song

Composed for the opening of the John F. Kennedy Center for the Performing Arts in Washington, Mass unconventionally and innovatively combines liturgy in Latin and English with contemporary theatre. The score is also eclectic, with music for traditional boys choir, classical singers as well as rock singers, with rock musicians integrated into a traditional orchestra in the pit. The abstract story takes place during the celebration of a mass, and explores modern, personal issues of faith and experience. "A Simple Song" (A Hymn and Psalm) is sung by the Mass celebrant (originally a high lyric baritone) at the beginning of the show.

ON THE TOWN

Musical in two acts. Music by Leonard Bernstein. Lyrics by Betty Comden and Adolph Green. Book by Betty Comden and Adolph Green, based on an idea by Jerome Robbins. First performance: December 13, Boston. Broadway opening: December 28, 1944. Director of the original production: George Abbott. Choreographer: Jerome Robbins.

Selections:

I Feel Like I'm Not Out of Bed Yet

Lonely Town

Lucky to Be Me

Some Other Time

On the Town was the first Broadway musical success for a remarkable group of collaborators: Leonard Bernstein, lyricists/librettists Betty Comden and Adolph Green, and choreographer Jerome Robbins. Robbins and Bernstein had worked together in early 1944 on their ballet *Fancy Free*, which chronicled the one-day shore leave of three sailors in New York. By the spring they realized this material would make great musical comedy. Bernstein asked Comden and Green, his friends from a little known night-club act, to write the lyrics and book for the show. Veteran George Abbott directed the project. Bernstein wrote an entirely new score, not using any music from *Fancy Free*. Besides many inventive songs, the score featured musical passages that highlighted dazzling choreography by Robbins, which helped to further elevate the stature of dance on the Broadway stage. These interludes also showed Bernstein's unique, substantial theatre styles as a composer. Comden and Green brought their comic timing into their writing, realizing their own words in portraying the characters Claire and Ozzie onstage.

An American navy ship docks in New York during World War II. In the early morning a longshoreman sings **"I Feel Like I'm Not Out of Bed Yet."** Three wide-eyed sailors disembark into the big city for the first time. They plan to cram their 24-hour shore leave full of sightseeing and skirt-chasing. Chip wants to see all the sights, and Ozzie wants to meet some women. Gabey spies a poster of Ivy Smith in the subway, the new "Miss Turnstiles," the non-celebrity status of a young woman chosen to decorate the subway platforms each month. He immediately falls for her and takes the poster off the wall (a move which will start the police looking for him). His buddies Ozzie and Chip forego their own plans to help Gabey track her down. Along the way all three get sidetracked in a travelogue around New York. Ozzie wanders into the Museum of Natural History looking for Miss Turnstiles and bumps into an anthropologist, Claire, who is as interested in modern man (particularly his physique) as she is in ancient man. Not making any progress, Gabey feels lonesome in the big city and sings **"Lonely Town."** By shear coincidence he recognizes Ivy, who is $50 in debt to her voice teacher. Ivy agrees to meet Gabey later, but her greedy voice teacher threatens her and insists she sing that night in a job at the amusement park at Coney Island. Chip finds he doesn't need the sight-seeing map given to him by his father after encountering boy-crazy lady cabbie, Hildy, who takes him back to her apartment. Gabey sings **"Lucky to Be Me"** in Times Square waiting for Ivy, not knowing that she is unable to meet him because she must perform at Coney Island. Gabey, his friends and their new girlfriends head to Coney Island to find Ivy, but are chased by the police. The two new couples, Claire and Ozzie, Hildy and Chip, realize their time together is running out in **"Some Other Time"** (originally a quartet, adapted as a solo for this edition). In the morning the sailors are "escorted" by New York's finest back to their ship.

The 1949 film version directed by Gene Kelly and Stanley Donen discarded most of Bernstein's score, retaining: "I Feel Like I'm Not Out of Bed Yet," "New York, New York" (adapted), "Miss Turnstiles Dance" (adapted), "Come Up to My Place," "A Day in New York Ballet" (adapted from "Times Square Ballet"), "Lonely Town," "Pas de Deux," and "Subway Ride and Imaginary Coney Island." Robbins' original choreography was replaced by Kelly and Donen.

WEST SIDE STORY

Musical in two acts. Music by Leonard Bernstein. Lyrics by Stephen Sondheim. Book by Arthur Laurents, loosely based on Shakespeare's *Romeo and Juliet*, based on a concept of Jerome Robbins. First performance: August 19, 1957, Washington, D.C. Broadway opening: September 26, 1957. Original production directed and choreographed by Jerome Robbins.

Selections:

Jet Song

Maria

Cool

The origins of *West Side Story* can be traced to early 1949. Jerome Robbins, who had conceived *On the Town*, approached Leonard Bernstein about a re-imagining and updating of *Romeo and Juliet*. The initial concept involved a Jewish boy and an Italian Catholic girl on New York's lower east side. Bernstein was interested, along with Arthur Laurents, but Bernstein had other commitments. In 1955 the three picked up the idea again, changing the players in the tale to reflect the mid-1950s mood and the issues over Puerto Rican immigration into the city. With the idea of rival gangs, moved to the New York neighborhood of gang activity at the time, *West Side Story* was off and running. A young Stephen Sondheim was brought in to write lyrics. The authors tried to usher in a new kind of American drama with *West Side Story*, not quite opera, but not quite traditional Broadway musical, with a stronger emphasis on character and dance. Bernstein later stated, "I don't consider it an opera. I think it has operatic qualities and moments, but it's not an opera because it is basically spoken dialogue scenes interspersed with music, even though it's much more interspersed than the average… I think what distinguishes *West Side Story* from other musicals is the copious use of dance, and this provides simply twice as much music as you ordinarily hear."

The show portrays a struggle for the streets of New York between two gangs. The Jets, a group of self-styled "American" teenagers, are led by Riff. The Sharks, Puerto Rican newcomers, are led by the fiery Bernardo. This bitter rivalry has deep seeds in racial prejudice and cultural insensitivity. The musical opens with **"Jet Song"** sung by Riff and the Jets (adapted here in an abbreviated solo version). Both the Sharks and the Jets and their girls attend a dance at a school gym, where Tony meets and falls in love at first sight with Maria, Bernardo's sister. Reeling with emotion he sings **"Maria."** The Jets nervously wait for a war council at Doc's drugstore. Riff settles them down with **"Cool"** before the Sharks arrive. A plan for a showdown rumble is made between the two gangs. Tony persuades them that it will be a fair fistfight rather than something more violent with weapons. That evening things get out of hand at the rumble. Bernardo draws a switchblade and fatally stabs Riff. Impulsively acting in shock, grief and anger Tony stabs and kills Bernardo in instant revenge.

Tony comes to Maria, anguished. Maria's love for him wins over her grief for her brother's death. They dream of a safe and peaceful place, which appears in a ballet sequence. Tony slips away. Anita reluctantly agrees to take a message for Maria, detained by police for questioning, to Tony at Doc's drugstore, where she is manhandled and nearly raped by the Jets. In anger she lies and tells them that Chino has found out about Tony and Maria, and has killed Maria. Unconsolable at the news, Tony rushes in the street, yelling for Chino to shoot him. Just as he sees Maria a shot rings out, and Tony soon lies dying in Maria's arms.

Most of the score was retained for the 1961 film version of the musical, although there were drastic shifts in song and scene order.

WONDERFUL TOWN

Musical in two acts. Music by Leonard Bernstein. Lyrics by Betty Comden and Adolph Green. Book by Joseph A. Fields and Jerome Chodorov, based on their play *My Sister Eileen*. First performance: January 19, 1953, New Haven, Connecticut. Broadway opening: February 26, 1953.

Selection:

A Quiet Girl

It's Love

The 1940 play *My Sister Eileen* was based on semi-autobiographical stories by Ruth McKenney that appeared in *The New Yorker*. Rosalind Russell played the role of Ruth Sherwood in the 1942 Columbia Pictures movie of *My Sister Eileen*. A few years later the musical *Wonderful Town* was written as a stage vehicle for her. Initially other writers were engaged. When they failed to impress the producers, Bernstein, Comden and Green were brought in to write music and lyrics. Under pressure to finish before the producer's option on Russell's contract expired, the team turned out the score in four weeks.

In the 1930s Ruth and Eileen are two sisters making their way in Greenwich Village, having recently moved from Ohio. Ruth is trying to be a writer (she has a typewriter, at least), and Eileen struggles to become an actress (her principal talent is that she's pretty). Ruth's potential editor at the *Manhatter*, Bob Baker, tells her she should move back west before he even looks at her writing. After reading her stories he comes to see Ruth at home to apologize for being curt, and instead encounters Eileen, who immediately falls a little bit in love with him. Bob has feelings too, revealed in **"A Quiet Girl."** Later, Eileen realizes that Ruth loves Bob, and suddenly Bob realizes, despite wanting a quiet girl, he's in love with the boisterous Ruth (**"It's Love"**). Ruth and Bob find one another, and forbidding New York has turned out to be a wonderful town.

A Simple Song
from *Mass*
original key: a whole step higher

Lyrics by
STEPHEN SCHWARTZ and
LEONARD BERNSTEIN

Music by
LEONARD BERNSTEIN

*Repeat if acoustically necessary

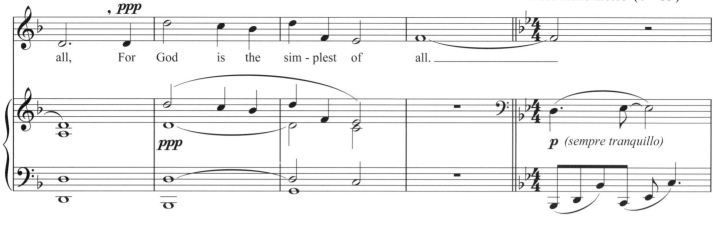

lift up my voice ___ to the Lord ___ Sing-ing Lau-da, Lau dē. ___ For the

Lord ___ is my shade, Is the shade up-on my ___ right hand, ___ And the

sun shall not smite ___ me by day ___ Nor the moon ___ by night. ___

Bless-ed is the man who loves the Lord, Lau - da, Lau - da,

Lau - dē, And walks in His ways.

Cadenza (freely)

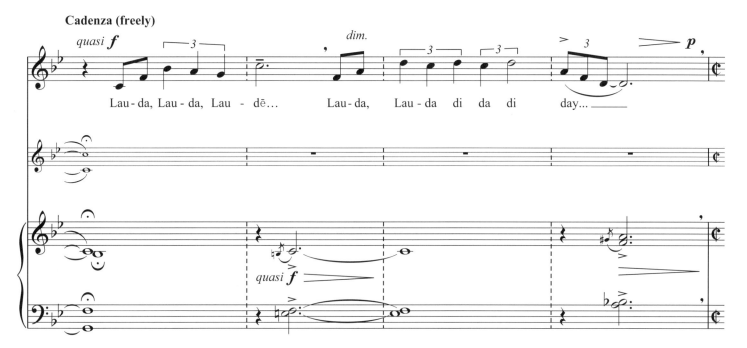

Lau - da, Lau - da, Lau - dē... Lau - da, Lau - da di da di day...

A tempo (più lento)

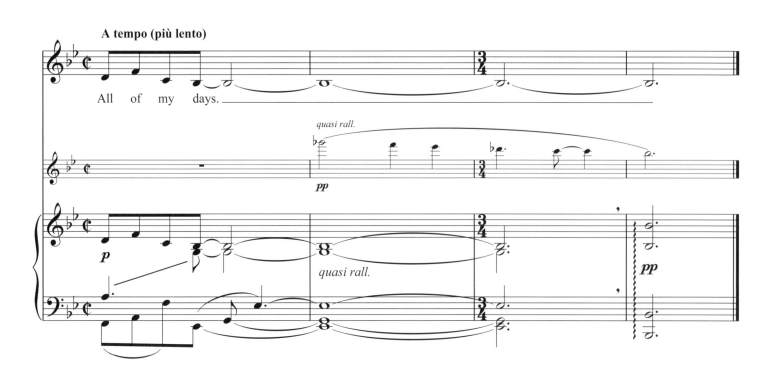

All of my days.

Flute

A Simple Song
from *Mass*
original key: a whole step higher

Lyrics by
STEPHEN SCHWARTZ and
LEONARD BERNSTEIN

Music by
LEONARD BERNSTEIN

Tranquillo ♩ = 48

Poco meno mosso (♩ = 88)

I will sing His prais-es   while I live

p

5

[p]

pp

(pn.)

Solo

espr.

[p]

molto rall. e dim.

A tempo (più lento)

All of my days.

pp, *quasi rall.*

This part may be carefully cut from the book.

I Feel Like I'm Not Out of Bed Yet

from *On the Town*

original key

Lyrics by
BETTY COMDEN and ADOLPH GREEN

Music by
LEONARD BERNSTEIN

Sleep in your la - dy's arms. _____ I

left my old wo - man still sleep - ing.

Mmm, _____ Oh, the air is

sweet, but my wo - man's sweet - er. _ Sleep, sleep in your

la - dy's arms. Sleep in your la - dy's arms. _____ All

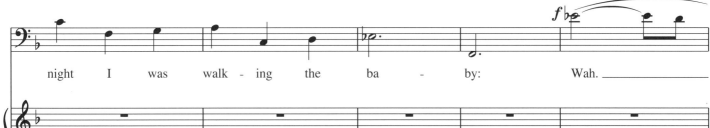

night I was walk - ing the ba - by: Wah. _____

Oh, his eyes are blue, but her eyes are blu - er. _

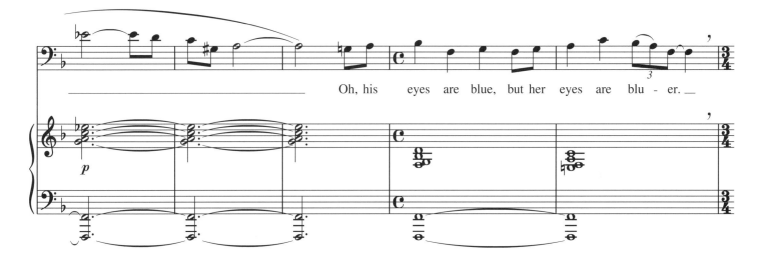

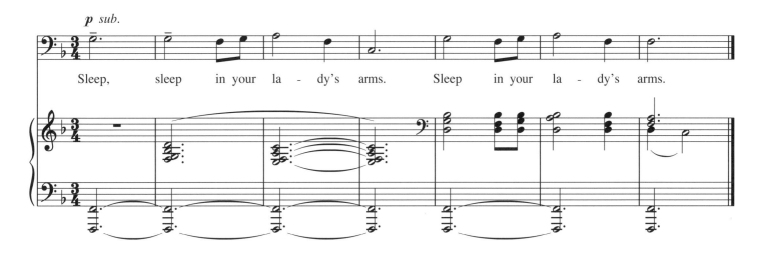

Sleep, sleep in your la - dy's arms. Sleep in your la - dy's arms.

Lonely Town
from *On the Town*
original key

Lyrics by
BETTY COMDEN and ADOLPH GREEN

Music by
LEONARD BERNSTEIN

* The verse here, different from the show version, was written for a stand-alone concert version of the song.

on Broad - way, If you're a - lone they are both the same.

In tempo
Fast, with urgency

A town's a lone - ly town, When you pass through And there is no one wait - ing there for you, Then it's a lone - ly town. You wan - der

up and down, The crowds rush by, A mil - lion

fa - ces pass be - fore your eye, Still it's a lone - ly town.

Un - less there's love, A love that's shin - ing like a har - bor light,

light, You're lost in the night; Un - less there's

love, The world's an emp-ty place _____ And ev-'ry

town's _____ a lone-ly town. _____

Un-less there's

Lucky to Be Me

from *On the Town*

original key

Lyrics by
BETTY COMDEN and ADOLPH GREEN

Music by
LEONARD BERNSTEIN

This song is for Gabey and chorus, adapted as a solo for this edition.

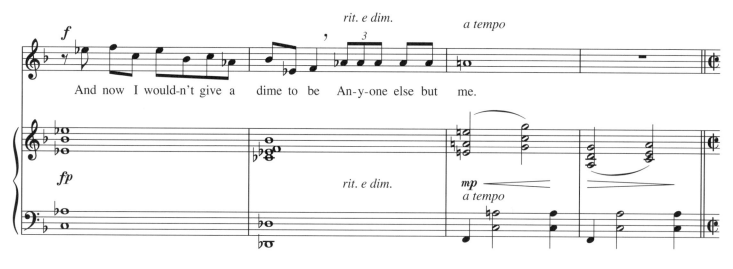

And now I would-n't give a dime to be An-y-one else but me.

Gently (♩ = 60)

What a day, For - tune smiled and came my way, Bring - ing love I

nev - er thought I'd see, I'm so luck - y to be me.

What a night, Sud - den - ly you came in sight, Look - ing just the

way I'd hoped you'd be, I'm so luck-y to be me.

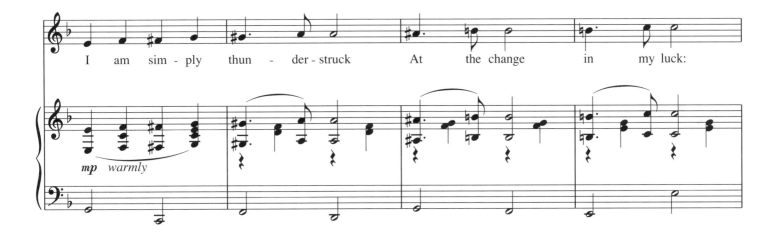

I am sim-ply thun-der-struck At the change in my luck:

Knew at once I want-ed you, Nev-er dreamed you'd want me too.

I'm so proud You chose me from all the crowd, There's no oth-er

guy I'd rath - er be, I could laugh out loud, I'm so luck - y to be

me.

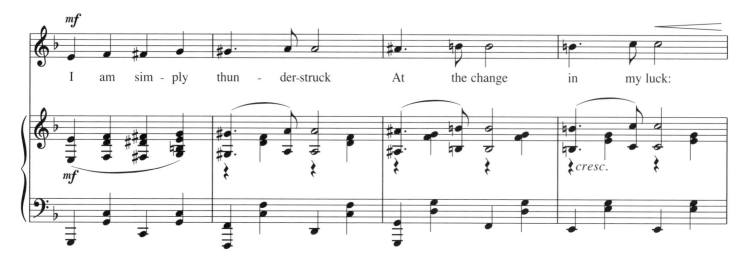

I am sim - ply thun - der-struck At the change in my luck:

Some Other Time

from *On the Town*

original key: a whole step higher

Lyrics by
BETTY COMDEN and ADOLPH GREEN

Music by
LEONARD BERNSTEIN

Begun by Claire, this song becomes a quartet in the show for Claire, Hildy, Chip and Ozzie. Adapted as a solo for this edition.

This day was just a to - ken, Too man - y words are still un - spo - ken.

Oh, well, we'll catch up Some oth - er time. _____ Just when the fun is

start - ing, Comes the time for part - ing, But let's be glad for what we've had And

what's to come. There's so much more em - brac - ing Still to be done, but

time is rac - ing. Oh, well, we'll catch up Some oth - er time. _____

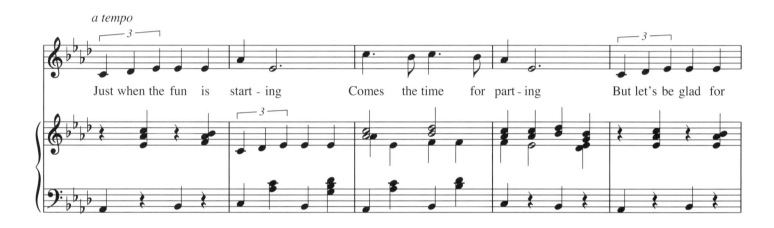

a tempo

Just when the fun is start - ing Comes the time for part - ing But let's be glad for

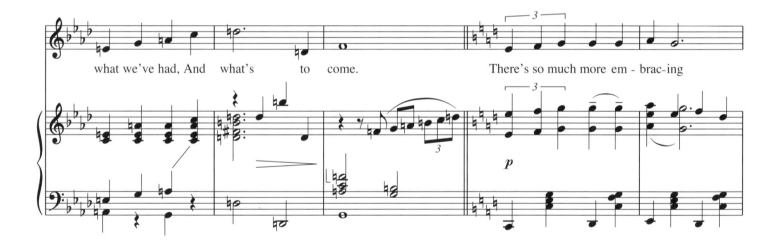

what we've had, And what's to come. There's so much more em - brac - ing

Still to be done, but time is rac - ing, Oh, well, We'll catch up Some oth - er time. _____

Cool

from *West Side Story*

original key

Lyrics by
STEPHEN SONDHEIM

Music by
LEONARD BERNSTEIN

"Cool" is an extended dance number, with the Jets entering to sing at the end, adapted here as a solo, using Riff's opening section.

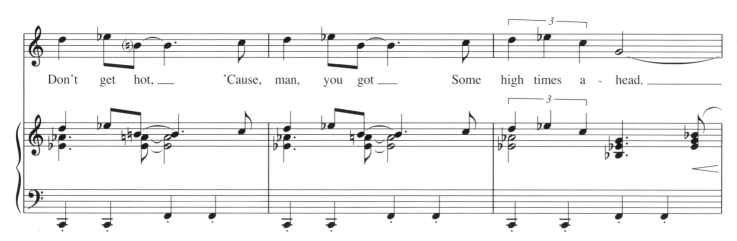

Don't get hot, __ 'Cause, man, you got __ Some high times a - head. __

__ Take it slow __ and, Dad - dy - o, __ You can live it up and die in bed! __

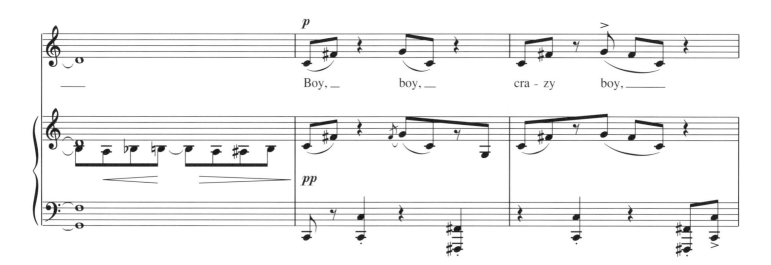

Boy, __ boy, __ cra - zy boy, __

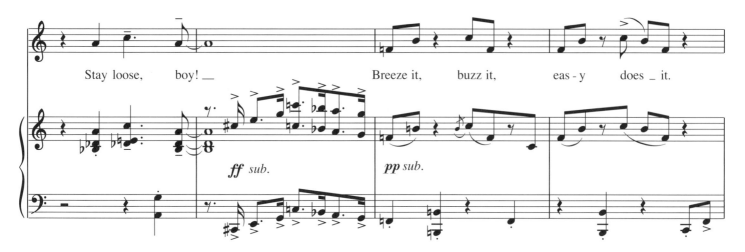

Stay loose, boy! __ Breeze it, buzz it, eas - y does __ it.

Turn off the juice, _____ boy. Go, man, go, ___ But

not like a yo - yo school - boy. _____ Just ___ play it

cool, boy, _____ Real ___ cool! _____

Jet Song
from *West Side Story*
original key

Lyrics by
STEPHEN SONDHEIM

Music by
LEONARD BERNSTEIN

Allegro moderato (deliberately) ♩. = 116-128

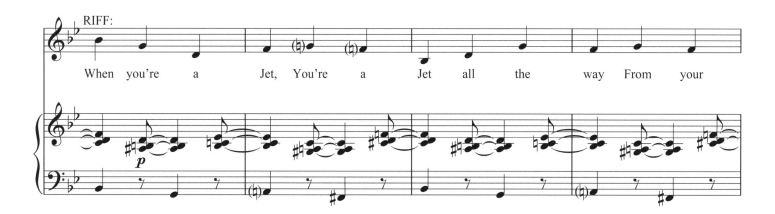

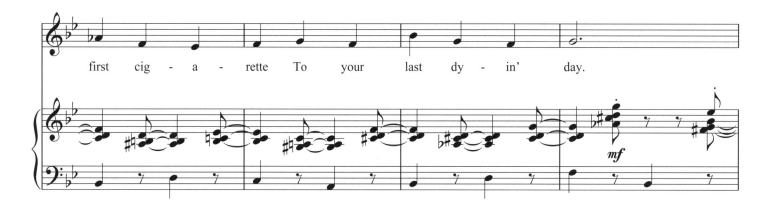

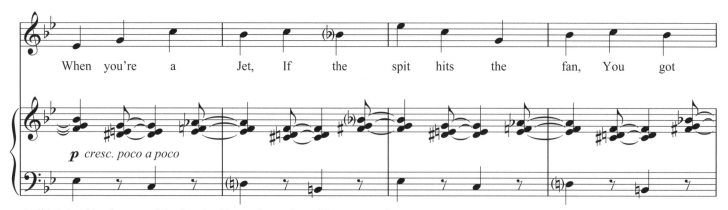

Riff is joined by the rest of the Jets in this number, adapted here as a solo.

*Play this chord with the thumb covering two notes: C double-sharp (D) and E; the 2 finger is on D-sharp, 4 on A-sharp, 5 on B.

set With a cap - i - tal J, Which you'll nev - er for -

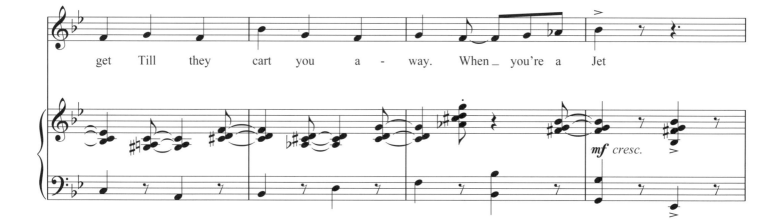

get Till they cart you a - way. When you're a Jet

you stay a Jet! _____

Maria

from *West Side Story*

original key: a major third higher

Lyrics by
STEPHEN SONDHEIM

Music by
LEONARD BERNSTEIN

* Original Broadway production: The repeated "Marias" were sung by off-stage voices.

ri - a! ____ Say it loud and there's mu - sic play - ing, Say it

soft and it's al - most like pray - ing. ____ Ma - ri - a, ____ I'll

nev - er stop say - ing Ma - ri - a, ____ Ma -

ri - a, ____ Ma - ri - a, Ma - ri -

It's Love
from *Wonderful Town*
original key

Lyrics by
BETTY COMDEN and ADOLPH GREEN

Music by
LEONARD BERNSTEIN

this is love, Then why have I fought it? _____ What a

way to feel! I could touch the sky. _____ What a

way to feel, I'm a dif-f'rent guy! _____ It's

love! At last, I've some-one to cheer for! _____ It's

love! At last I've learned what we're here for. _____ I've

Broadly

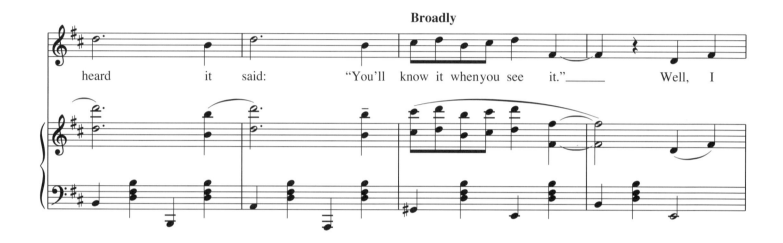

heard it said: "You'll know it when you see it." _____ Well, I

rall. *a tempo*

see it, I know it, It's love! _____

La da dee da da da. _____ Love! _____

La da dee da da da. What a way to feel! I could

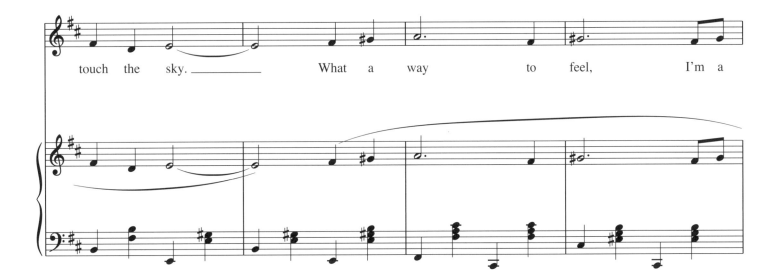

touch the sky. _____ What a way to feel, I'm a

dif - f'rent guy! _____ It's love! At last, I've

48

some-one to cheer for! _____ It's love, At last, I've

learned what we're here for. _____ I've heard it said: "You'll

Broadly *rall.* **Maestoso** *opt.*

know it when you see it." ___ Well, I see it, I know it, It's love! _____

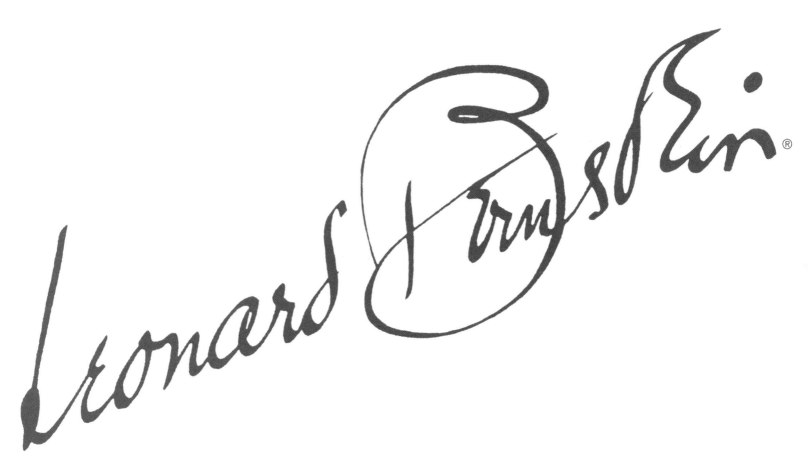

This page intentionally left blank to facilitate page turns.

A Quiet Girl

from *Wonderful Town*
original key

Lyrics by
BETTY COMDEN and ADOLPH GREEN

Music by
LEONARD BERNSTEIN

Suddenly calm

Andante (♩ = 60)

An-oth-er kind, a dif-f'rent kind of girl? _____

Slowly and simply, like a folksong

I love a qui-et girl, _ I love a gen-tle girl, _

Warm as sun - light, Soft, soft as snow.

Her smile, a ten-der smile, _ Her voice, a vel-vet voice, _

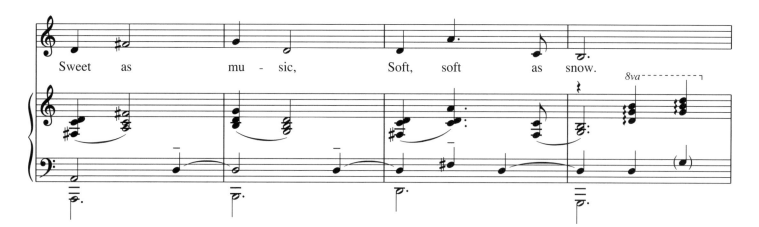

Sweet as mu - sic, Soft, soft as snow.

More flowing [*a bit quicker*]

When she is near me the world's in re - pose.

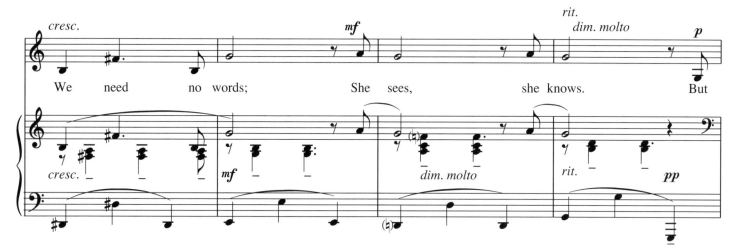

We need no words; She sees, she knows. But

Tempo I

Where is my qui - et girl? _ Where is my gen - tle girl? _

Where is the spe-cial girl, __ Who is soft, soft as snow?

Some - where, some - where, my qui - et girl.

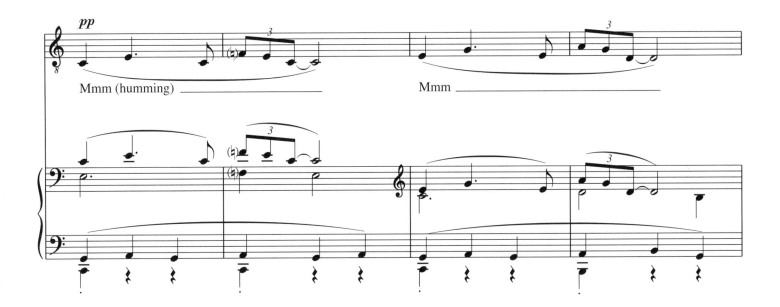

Mmm (humming) _____ Mmm _____

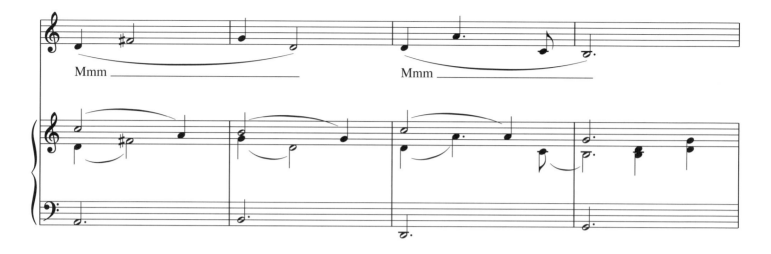

Mmm _____ Mmm _____

More flowing

When she is near me the world's in re - pose.

We need no words; She sees, she knows. But

Tempo I

where is my qui-et girl? __ Where is my gen-tle girl? __

Where is the spe-cial girl, __ Who is soft, soft as snow? Some-where,

some-where, My qui-et girl. _____